Michio Kaku

by Michelle Parkin

NORWOOD HOUSE PRESS

Cover: Michio Kaku loves sharing his ideas on science and the future.

Norwood House Press
For information regarding Norwood House Press, please visit our website at: www.norwoodhousepress.com or call 866-565-2900.

PHOTO CREDITS: Cover, ©Sam Aronov/Getty Images; 5, ©Matthew Corley/Shutterstock; 6, ©General Photographic Agency / Stringer/Getty Images; 9, ©Ronald Patrick / Stringer/Getty Images; 11, ©John Penney/Shutterstock; 13, ©David Becker / Stringer/ Getty Images; 14, ©Patrick McMullan / Contributor/Getty Images; 17, ©Amy Sussman / Stringer/Getty Images; 18, ©Ser Amantio di Nicolao/Wikimedia; 21, ©PictureGroup/ Sipa USA/Newscom

Hardcover ISBN: 978-1-68450-743-6
Paperback ISBN: 978-1-68404-823-6

Library of Congress Cataloging-in-Publication Data

Names: Parkin, Michelle, author.
Title: Michio Kaku / by Michelle Parkin.
Description: [Chicago] : Norwood House Press, [2023] | Series: Stem superstars | Includes index. | Audience: Ages 5-8 | Audience: Grades K-1 | Summary: "Describes the life and work of Michio Kaku, a theoretical physicist and futurist who works to popularize science"-- Provided by publisher.
Identifiers: LCCN 2022041779 (print) | LCCN 2022041780 (ebook) | ISBN 9781684507436 (hardcover) | ISBN 9781684048236 (paperback) | ISBN 9781684048434 (epub)
Subjects: LCSH: Kaku, Michio. | Physicists--United States--Biography--Juvenile literature.
Classification: LCC QC16.K19 P37 2023 (print) | LCC QC16.K19 (ebook) | DDC 530/.092--dc23/eng/20220831
LC record available at https://lccn.loc.gov/2022041779
LC ebook record available at https://lccn.loc.gov/2022041780

359N–012023
Manufactured in the United States of America in North Mankato, Minnesota.

★ Table of Contents ★

Chapter 1

Early Life

Michio Kaku was born on January 24, 1947. He grew up in California. His family didn't have much money.

Kaku was born in San Jose, California.

Albert Einstein lived from 1879 to 1955.

Kaku loved science. He looked up to Albert Einstein. Kaku learned all about his life and work.

In high school, Kaku was interested in **atoms**. He made a machine. It sped atoms along a wire. They smashed into each other. It was a small **particle accelerator**. It was made of 400 pounds (180 kilograms) of metal. There were 22 miles (35 kilometers) of copper wire. Kaku entered it in a science fair. He won!

The biggest particle accelerator is 17 miles (27 kilometers) long.

Chapter 2

Big Ideas

Kaku went to Harvard University. He studied **physics**. Kaku did well. Later, he went to the University of California, Berkeley. Then Kaku became a teacher at City College in New York.

Kaku has taught at City College for more than 45 years.

Did You Know?
Kaku thinks people might live on Mars one day.

Kaku has lots of ideas. Many are about the future. He talks about new science discoveries. He explains how they could change lives.

Kaku makes guesses about the future. He is a "futurist."

Kaku now lives in New York with his wife. They have two daughters.

Kaku is famous for his **theory**. It is called string field theory. It says the tiny bits that make up atoms are not like spots. They are like strings. This is one way to explain the universe.

Chapter 3

Science Speaker

Kaku wants others to get excited about science. He shares what it can be used for. He travels the world talking about it.

Kaku knows a lot about science. He explains it so everyone can understand.